BUNNIES BY THE BAY

MEETS LITTLE QUILTS

Suzanne Knutson • Krystal Kirkpatrick

Alice Berg • Mary Ellen Von Holt • Sylvia Johnson

Martingale
& COMPANY

BOTHELL, WASHINGTON

Bunnies By The Bay Meets Little Quilts

©1999 by Suzanne Knutson, Krystal Kirkpatrick, Alice Berg, Mary Ellen Von Holt, and Sylvia Johnson

Martingale & Company
PO Box 118
Bothell, WA 98041-0118 USA

Printed in Hong Kong

MISSION STATEMENT

WE ARE DEDICATED TO PROVIDING QUALITY PRODUCTS AND SERVICE BY WORKING TOGETHER TO INSPIRE CREATIVITY AND TO ENRICH THE LIVES WE TOUCH.

Library of Congress Cataloging-in-Publication Data

Bunnies by the bay meets little quilts
   / Suzanne Knutson . . . [et al.].
       p.   cm.
     ISBN 1-56477-281-0 (hardcover).
     —ISBN 1-56477-257-8 (pbk.)
     1. Patchwork—Patterns.
     2. Quilting—Patterns.   3. Miniature quilts.
   I. Knutson, Suzanne,.
   TT835.B795   1999
   746.46'041—dc21
                                          99-18471
                                             CIP

Credits
President: Nancy J. Martin
CEO/Publisher: Daniel J. Martin
Associate Publisher: Jane Hamada
Editorial Director: Mary V. Green
Design and Production Manager: Cheryl Stevenson
Technical Editing: Ursula Reikes
Editing and Design: Watershed Books
Photography: Brent Kane
Illustration: Laurel Strand
Bunnies By The Bay Original Art: Chris Theiss
Bunnies By The Bay Text: Suzanne Knutson

Contents

Bunnies By The Bay

Welcome to Bunnies By The Bay. We hope you are delighted with our first book from front to back,

back to front, or however you wish to read it. As sisters, we have always been close and shared a

sense of whimsy and mischief. When we first brought our handmade bunnies to sell at a Northwest

arts fair over thirteen years ago, we were amazed and happy to find that lots of other people felt the

same affection for our fuzzy little characters that we did. In fact, we sold out our entire stock of

bunnies in the very first day of the two-day event!

Today, our bunnies—and Emerson Duck (who has his own fan club!), kitties, and other cuddly friends—are still handcrafted, with loving attention paid to the smallest details and accessories that make each one unique. A row of antique pearl buttons, tiny wooden clogs fitting for a duck, a silk chiffon apron for an especially feminine bunny, or tea-dyed fabrics that give a feeling of timelessness to the outfits all help define each character's personality. Krys's work space is forever brimming with little antique collectibles, colorful ribbons, fabrics, and other inspirations that help us shape each new edition.

The scenes in this book that feature our little friends were all staged inside and outside the two turn-of-the-century houses in Anacortes and La Conner, Washington, that serve as homes and retail outlets for the bunnies and their friends. Here, you can enter the storied world of the bunnies and find everything from the latest editions of the bunnies (in the current season's theme fashions) to the carrot jams that we know the bunnies just love. And if you want to visit our bunny workshop in Anacortes, we'd love to greet you and show you what they've been up to lately. Our tours are fun—and we dare you to spend any time around the bunnies without imagining new stories for them!

For those of you who know the joy of sewing beautiful creations, we hope the bunnies, their friends, and the lovely quilts by Little Quilts will inspire you to create your own special projects. We can only say that by following our hearts and our bunnies, we have found a world of work that keeps us constantly at play.

We do have to admit the only part of making this book that was a tad frustrating is the fact that it isn't a storybook. The bunnies have so many tales to be told, and it was very difficult to keep them from taking over the book. I'm sure you'll be wondering if our tiny friend Clovis has learned to waddle quicker in her wooden clogs or if our little garden friends will learn the difficult lesson of waiting their turn for the wheelbarrow ride. In the meantime, we hope that spending the day with Bunnies By The Bay is always a story in itself. Enjoy!

5

SUZANNE KNUTSON   **KRYSTAL KIRKPATRICK**

Little Quilts

We never grew up! What we do today actually began when we were little girls. Each of us grew up in

different parts of the country and eventually ended up in the Atlanta area, where we met through our

quilting interest. It's interesting how people are brought together in friendship, and how creative

minds inspire each other into seeing dreams happen. Making little quilts to resemble the antique doll

quilts seen in country decorating magazines and books was the beginning. Several hundred little

reproductions were carefully stitched from scraps of fabric, tea-dyed, and sold to anxious buyers at

antique shows in the area. People began to collect these "textile paintings," and soon we realized that

it would be impossible to make enough little quilts for everyone in the world to have one.

It occurred to us that perhaps there were many admirers who would like to make their own, but were unsure of how to get our look. Kits that included everything except a needle, thread, and time were the next product, followed by patterns for quilters wishing to use their own fabrics. One idea led to the next, and, since 1984, Little Quilts has grown up to become a "real" business with customers worldwide.

On a peg, on the wall, by a bear, over a chair, or on a table . . . there are endless ways to use a little quilt to decorate a home. Magazine photographs often show antique doll quilts displayed in wonderful room settings, but trying to find a small quilt to use in our own rooms was difficult. The books and patterns from Little Quilts enable someone to make a reproduction using simple sewing skills. Because these quilts are meant to resemble those made or used by children, they need not be perfect. Beginners and advanced quilters enjoy the simplicity of the project, but the end result becomes a treasured and much-used heirloom.

Over the years we have been asked to open a retail store in our area. We came close a few times, but it just wasn't the right time. When we were invited to provide the quilt projects for this book, our lives changed.

We have always admired Bunnies By The Bay and share many similarities in what we do.

While in the Seattle area for a college graduation, Alice took a side trip to see Bunnies By The Bay. Their charming retail stores and workplace were an inspiration to us, and Little Quilts decided to open a retail store at last. It was meant to be! A perfect location opened up and we moved to an old, two-story building with pine floors and just the look we wanted. Featuring quilting, rug hooking, stitchery, gifts, and furniture . . . it truly is "Little Quilt Land."

Although many miles separate us on the continent, we feel that we have very special friends at Bunnies By The Bay. They have inspired us as a business, and once again proven that little ideas can become bigger ideas, bringing enjoyment to the lives of others near and far. It was our sincere pleasure to have been part of a book featuring the fabulous talent of Suzanne and Krystal. Enjoy making the quilt projects shown in the book, and as we have always said, "Everyone needs a quilt!"— even bunnies.

7

SYLVIA JOHNSON, ALICE BERG, MARY ELLEN VON HOLT

In the
GARDEN

"Whoops! Now that's what happens when we don't wait our turn,"
Pansy kindly warned her little garden helpers as they tumbled from the broken wheelbarrow.

Shoe Peg whispers to each ripe apple, as she gingerly polishes them to a beautiful shine, "You'll be apple butter, and this one a yummy pie, but the sweetest one of all is this apple of my eye!"

Our little family of country gardeners is clothed in fabrics, trims, and treasures we've acquired from our travels. The child's leather boots that Shoe Peg, our little hare, is showing off were discovered before sunrise at an outdoor swap meet in Pennsylvania.

Pansy is wearing a small child's well-worn, soft homespun checked dress and lace pinafore apron, found at a teddy bear show in San Diego. Buggy, Bumble, and Shoe Peg are dressed in their overalls and long dress made from old cutter quilts. To add intrigue, Krys included antique fruits, faded velvet flowers, and ribbons.

$\mathcal{B}$UMBLEBEE

MATERIALS

- 2½" of ½"-wide ribbon

- Embroidery floss or thread to match ribbon

- Small amount of polyester fiberfill for stuffing

- 1 black stamen

- Black embroidery floss

- Embroidery needle

- 1 white flower with 5 or 6 petals (approximately 1" diameter)

- Craft glue

- 10" of black wire (30 gauge)

12

The tiniest details on an outfit are the most charming, like the embroidered ladybug crawling up Picket's striped overalls or this buzzing bumblebee on Bumble's overalls.

DIRECTIONS

Step 1 – Fold ends of the 2½" piece of ribbon toward the middle so they overlap. Sew the ends together to make a loop. With the seam in the middle, flatten the loop.

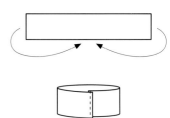

Step 2 – Sew together the long edges of one side of the loop, using a small overcast stitch.

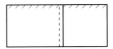

Step 3 – Fill the loop with a small amount of stuffing.

Step 4 – Sew together the remaining long edges of the loop.

Step 5 – Gather and tie off each end so the loop is now oval shaped. This is the bee body.

Step 6 – Fold the stamen in half and stitch to the under-side of the body to make the antennae.

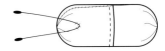

Bumble is as stumped as this old tree, mumbling,
"Now where could that busy bumblebee be?
Olly-olly-oxen free!"

Step 9 – Make a small loop at one end of the black wire. Glue the loop to the under-side of the body. Then, for fun, make a couple more loops in the wire.

Step 7 – Using 2 strands of black embroidery floss (about 24" long), wrap the floss around the middle of the body and tie a knot on the underside. Wrap the floss around the body 2 more times and stitch in place on the underside. Repeat to make 3 lines on the body.

Step 8 – Flatten the white flower (remove 1 petal if necessary—you need 5 petals). Glue the flower to the underside of the body so that 2 petals stick out on each side and 1 petal is at the end opposite the antennae.

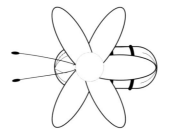

Summer Nine Patch Quilt

This bright and cheerful antique Nine Patch doll quilt was probably made from dress and apron fabrics. Reproduction fabrics available today make this easy to re-create.

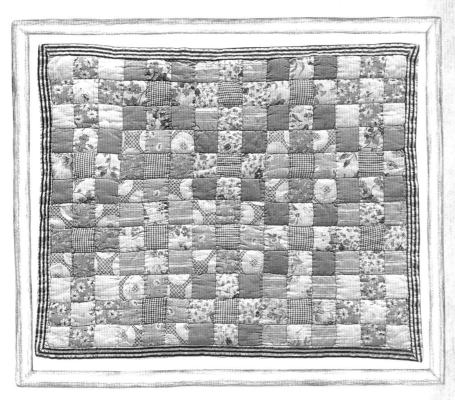

MATERIALS

- ½ yd. total assorted red, white, and blue prints, solids, and checks

- ⅛ yd. red-and-white stripe for border

- ¾ yd. for backing

- 19" x 23" piece of thin batting

DIRECTIONS

Measurements include ¹/₄"-wide seam allowances.

Step 1 – Cut 180 squares, each 1³/₄" x 1³/₄", from the assorted red, white, and blue fabrics.

(Or use the strip-piecing method shown on page 17, cutting strips 1³/₄" wide.)

FINISHED QUILT SIZE
17¹/₂" X 21¹/₄"

Step 2 – Arrange the squares into Nine Patch blocks and sew them together. Make 20 blocks.

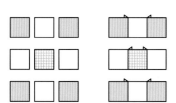

Step 3 – Sew the blocks together in 5 rows of 4, then join the rows to make the quilt top.

Step 4 – Cut 2 border strips, each $1^{3}/_{4}$" x 19 $^{1}/_{4}$", and sew to the sides. Cut 2 border strips, each $1^{3}/_{4}$" x $17^{1}/_{2}$", and sew to the top and bottom.

Step 5 – Layer the quilt top with batting and backing.

Step 6 – Baste and quilt as desired. We suggest quilting in-the-ditch between the squares.

Step 7 – Instead of a traditional binding, the border is turned over the raw edge of the quilt. Turn the edge of the border under ¹/₄". Fold the border to the back and hand stitch the folded edge of the border ¹/₄" from the raw edge of the quilt. There will be no batting in the piece of the border that is turned to the back.

Step 8 – Add a label.

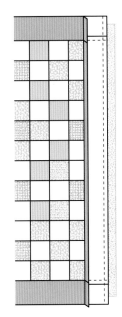
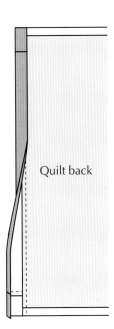

Quilt back

STRIP-PIECED NINE PATCH BLOCKS

The quilts in this book use either 1¹/₂"- or 1³/₄"-wide strips of fabric. Cut strips in random lengths from the fabrics. Sew the strips together as shown in threes. Press after the first two strips are joined, before adding the third in each set. Cut the segments into the size specified for each quilt. Sew them together into Nine Patch blocks.

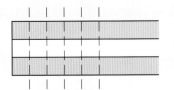
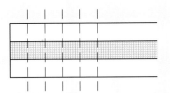
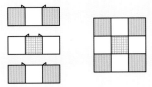

To Market, To Market
Jiggety-Jig

"Oh, Clovis, do speed it up. We're going to miss everything," her friends pleaded.

"I'm hurrying . . . I'm hurrying," Clovis quacked, completely out of breath, "But it's very hard in my waddle clogs!"

"Has anyone seen Clovis?
Gosh, I hope she's not still mad at us
for teasing her about her waddle clogs."

To MARKET, To MARKET

Dressing up for their once-a-week market trip means our friends wear finery made in turn-of-the-century laces, linens, and trims. For each unique outfit, Krys used elegant details with tatting and cutwork designs and an old hand-stitched cutter quilt in soft blues and creamy white. Hand-embroidered bees buzz on Clotilde's pinafore, and pale pink silk ribbon is woven through Chantilly's lace dress. Lacy Dutch-style hats show off everyone's ears—except Clovis, who has no ears to worry about.

Our little hare is waiting to fill her wagon with goodies and maybe a quilt or two. Painted upon the old wooden wagon is the saying, "Go often to the garden of thy friends, for weeds choke the unused path" (by Emerson . . . not the duck).

Market Bag

MATERIALS

- 6" x 14" piece of silk or vintage fabric

- 13" of lace trim

- 13" of medium rickrack

- 1 yd. of ⅛"-wide silk ribbon

- 1 plastic curtain ring, 1" diameter

- Small crochet hook

- Embroidery needle

- 2 different colors of embroidery floss to match silk

- 17 or 18 buttons, ⁵⁄₁₆" diameter

22

This little bag is called a beggar's pouch. The pattern was made from a vintage silk bag Krys found at an antique show. We used a vintage slip with rickrack crocheted along the edge, cutting it so the crocheted edge became the top of the purse.

DIRECTIONS

Step 1 – Cut a strip 1" x 6" from the short end of the piece of silk. Trim this to 1" x 4" for the ring loop. Turn the short ends of the ring loop under ¼". Fold the strip in half lengthwise, wrong sides together; press. Open the pressed strip and fold each long edge in

"How many buttons for your lovely quilt?"
Clotilde asked sweetly, as Clio pounced
and purred with pleasure upon the puffy coverlet.

toward the center fold and press again. Topstitch along both sides and ends.

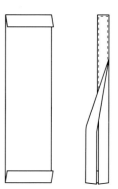

Step 2 – Fold one long edge of the 6" x 13" piece of silk under ¼". Fold under ¼" again and stitch. Sew the lace to the folded edge. Sew the rickrack to the top of the lace.

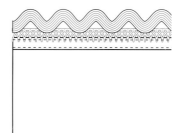

Step 3 – Sew a running stitch along the bottom of the bag. Gather the edge to 8".

Step 4 – Using the ¹/₈"-wide silk ribbon, single crochet around the plastic curtain ring to cover it.

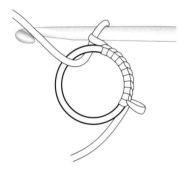

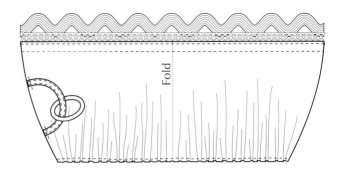

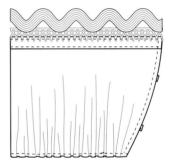

DECORATING THE BAG

Step 1 – Use 1 strand of embroidery floss to do a stem stitch along the center of the rickrack.

Step 2 – Sew buttons to the peaks of the rickrack, using the other color of embroidery floss. Embroider French knots above and below the stem stitch.

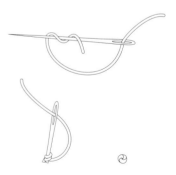

French Knot

Step 5 – Put the ring loop through the covered curtain ring. Pin the ends of the loop to one end of the bag, 1¹/₄" from the top and 1¹/₄" from the bottom. Fold the bag in half with right sides together. Make sure the ring loop is facing inside the bag. Sew across the bottom of the bag and up the side, using a ¹/₂"-wide seam. Turn the bag right side out.

24

LITTLE DOUBLE IRISH CHAIN QUILT

This small version of the traditional Double Irish Chain quilt is perfect for an antique doll bed or any tabletop.

MATERIALS

- ½ yd. medium blue print for blocks and binding

- ¼ yd. light print for blocks

- 1½ yds. muslin for blocks, border, and backing

- 23" x 33" piece of thin batting

DIRECTIONS

Measurements include ¹/₄"-wide seam allowances.

Step 1 – For Block A, cut the following squares, each 1½" x 1½":

- 96 medium blue print squares

- 72 light print squares
- 32 muslin squares

Step 2 – Arrange the squares to make Block A and sew

FINISHED QUILT SIZE
21¹/₂" X 31¹/₂"

them together. Make 8 blocks.

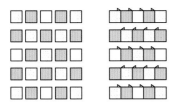

Step 3 – For Block B, cut the following pieces:

- 28 medium blue print squares, each $1^1/2$" x $1^1/2$"
- 28 muslin rectangles, each $1^1/2$" x $3^1/2$"
- 7 muslin squares, each $3^1/2$" x $3^1/2$"

Step 4 – Arrange the pieces to make Block B and sew them together. Make 7 blocks.

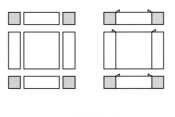

Step 5 – Arrange the A and B blocks in 5 rows of 3, alternating the blocks (see the photo on page 25). Sew the blocks together, then join the rows.

Step 6 – Cut 2 border strips, each $3^1/2$" x $15^1/2$", and sew to the top and bottom. Cut 2 border strips, each $3^1/2$" x $31^1/2$", and sew to the sides.

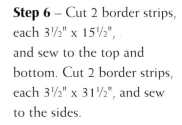

Step 7 – Layer the quilt top with batting and backing.

Step 8 – Baste and quilt as desired. We suggest cross-hatch lines through the center, feather plumes in the border, and flowers in the plain squares.

Step 9 – Bind the quilt and add a label.

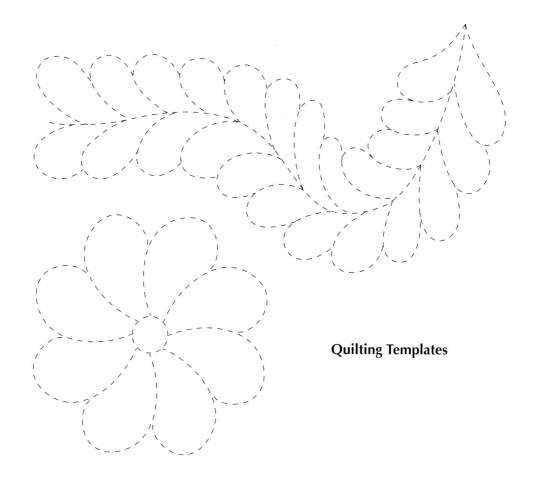

Quilting Templates

WASH DAY

"What is the first rule we learn when doing laundry?" Fancy asked her fellow felines.

Breezy piped up, "We never, never, never starch our tails, no matter how curled they may become."

"Whew! It's a good thing you had a bath, Buster,
so I could keep my socks clean while I rest my feet on you."

$\mathcal{W}$ASH $\mathcal{D}$AY

Krys enjoys creating her one-of-a-kind characters the most, because she has total freedom to use her found treasures and goodies to design truly individualized friends. Her wash-day kitties are a perfect example of what she can do when no restrictions apply. Each cat is delightfully outfitted in finds from weekend flea markets, early-morning swap meets, and special vintage clothing shows.

Wonderful old table linens, colorful embroidered tea towels, tattered doilies, old quilts, trims of rickrack, well-used cloth napkins, buttons, and vintage flowers bring these felines to life and make them utterly unique.

Yo-Yo Headband

MATERIALS

- 6" x 8" piece of fabric for yo-yos

- 3" x 5" piece of contrasting fabric for yo-yo centers

- 21" of $^3/_8$"-wide lace

- Small amount of polyester fiberfill for stuffing

- 3 buttons to cover, $^3/_8$" diameter

- 1$^1/_8$ yds. of $^1/_4$"-wide red plaid ribbon

- 2 daisies, approximately 1" diameter

- Craft glue

32

Our kitty's flowered headband can make a charming accessory for your favorite child or bunny.

DIRECTIONS

Step 1 – Cut 3 yo-yos from fabric, using the circle template on page 34. Cut the lace into 3 pieces, each 7" long. Use a running stitch to sew the lace to the right side of the fabric along the outside edge of the yo-yo circle, with the scalloped edge of the lace facing the center of the yo-yo. Do not cut the thread yet.

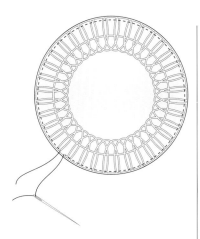

Step 2 – Pull the thread from the running stitch to gather the edges and form the yo-yo. Stuff the yo-yo with a small amount of fiberfill. Knot the thread and clip ends.

"Please throw me way up in the air, Bliss! I promise I'll land on my feet," Wispy begged.

Step 3 – Cover 3 buttons with the contrasting fabric, following package directions. Sew a covered button to the center of each yo-yo.

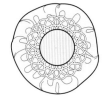

Step 4 – Cut the red plaid ribbon into 1 piece, 23" long, and 2 pieces, each 8½" long. Sew 1 yo-yo to the center of the 23"-long piece of ribbon. Sew each of the remaining yo-yos 2" from the center yo-yo.

Step 5 – Make a double bow from each 8½" piece of ribbon. Sew the bows between the yo-yos.

Step 6 – Glue a daisy to the center of each double bow.

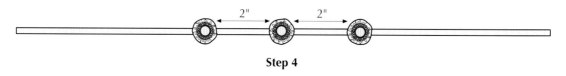

2"   2"

Step 4

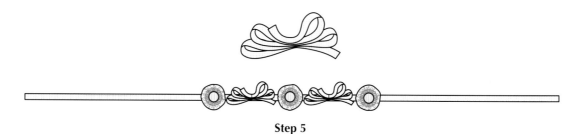

Step 5

Step 6

34

Yo-Yo Circle
Do not add
seam allowance.

FLOWERS IN THE GARDEN QUILT

The Grandmother's Flower Garden quilt block is everyone's favorite traditional quilt pattern! This antique little doll quilt was probably made from the leftover blocks of a larger quilt. Flowers are joined with a solid green fabric, often referred to as the "garden path." Make this small version for your favorite bunny!

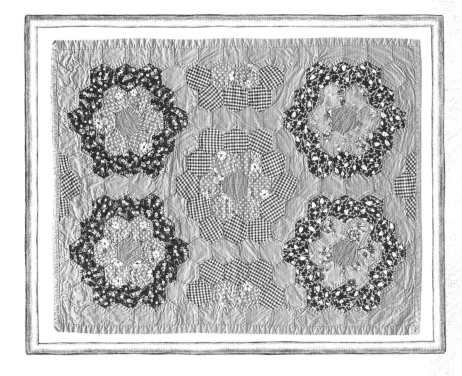

MATERIALS

- Template plastic

- Lightweight cardboard

- 6" x 8" piece of purple print for flower centers

- 1/2 yd. total assorted blue and green prints for flowers

- 1/2 yd. total assorted red prints for flowers

- 3/4 yd. green solid for garden path, backing, and binding

- 19" x 24" piece of thin batting

35

DIRECTIONS

Measurements include 1/4"-wide seam allowances.

Step 1 – Make a plastic template of the hexagon shape.

Trace and cut 205 hexagons from lightweight cardboard.

FINISHED QUILT SIZE
17 1/2" X 22 1/2"

Step 2 – Pin a cardboard hexagon to the wrong side of a piece of fabric. Cut around the shape, leaving a ¼"-wide seam allowance. Cut the following number of hexagons:

- 5 from purple print for centers
- 34 from blue and green prints for first round
- 76 from red prints for second round and partial flowers
- 86 from green solid for garden path

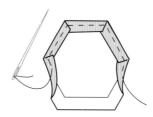

Step 3 – Fold the ¼"-wide seam allowance over the edge of the cardboard and baste.

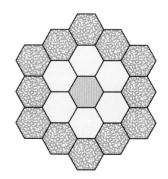

Step 4 – Whipstitch the hexagons together as shown to make 5 flowers and 4 partial flowers.

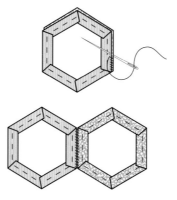

Step 5 – Join the flowers and partial flowers with the green solid hexagons. Refer to the photo for placement. Remove the basting and the cardboard.

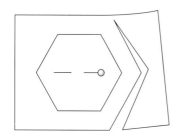

Make 5.

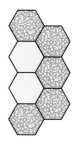

Make 2.

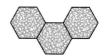

Make 2.

36

Step 6 – Press the quilt top and trim the sides and top and bottom to straighten the edges.

Step 7 – Layer the quilt top with batting and backing.

Step 8 – Baste and quilt as desired. We suggest quilting around the flowers and the garden path.

Step 9 – Bind the quilt and add a label.

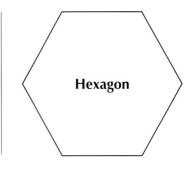

Hexagon

A HARE-O-WEEN Halloween Ball

"Oh, Emerson, don't be such a scaredy-cat. It's only me," little Tricksy giggled.

"That's easy for you to say, Tricksy. You *are* a cat!" the little duck grumbled.

"We must have gotten the wrong goody bags, Emerson.
Yuck, fruits and vegetables!"

Elegant, sophisticated, and thoroughly enchanting— it's no trick that this bunch is a wonderful treat for your eyes. A combination of beautiful black brocade, taffeta moiré, and rich velvets in midnight black and ripe pumpkin orange makes our group the "cat's meow," as Tricksy would say.

Trimmings from Europe include the satin braid, hand-dyed silk ribbons, wool felt, and vintage fruits and flowers. Intricate hand embroidery makes this a very bewitching group indeed!

41

Jack Pin

Materials

- 2" square of orange velveteen

- 2" square of green felt

- 2" square of fleece

- 1 button with a shank, 1¹/₈" diameter

- Black and green embroidery floss

- Embroidery needle

- 6" of thin green florist wire

42

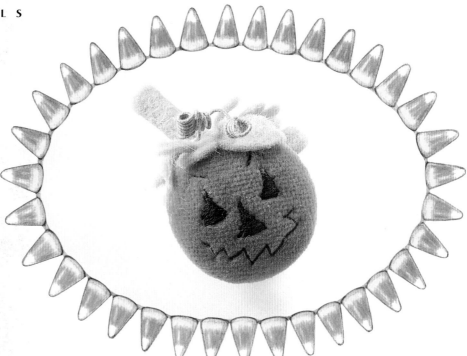

Making a unique pin out of a button is an easy way to accessorize a holiday outfit.

Directions

Step 1 – Using the templates on page 44, cut out the face from the velveteen, and the back, leaves, and stem from the felt.

Count Jackula holds still while his countess pins on his jack pin.
They're ready for a hare-raising time at the Halloween Ball.

Step 2 – Draw the face on the velveteen. Use black embroidery floss to stitch the face, making a satin stitch for the eyes and nose, and a backstitch for the mouth and eyebrows.

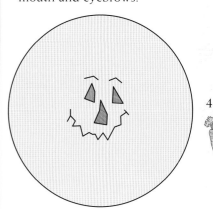

43

Step 3 – Place the square of fleece on the wrong side of the velveteen. Sew a running stitch along the outside edge to gather the velveteen around the button. Knot and clip the thread ends.

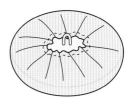

Step 4 – Make a small slit in the center of the green felt circle for the button shank to poke through. Stitch or glue the circle to the back of the button, covering the raw edges of the velveteen.

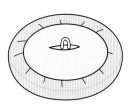

Step 6 – Wrap each end of the 6" floral wire around a large needle to make the coils. Attach to the base of the stem.

Step 7 – Use a safety pin to attach the pin, or sew it directly to the garment.

Step 5 – Roll the felt to make the stem. Stitch the leaves and stem to the top of the button with green embroidery floss.

Templates

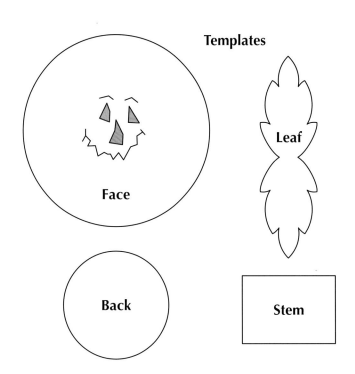

Face

Back

Leaf

Stem

$\mathcal{B}$UNNY HARVEST $\mathcal{Q}$UILT

For bunnies, fall is the perfect time to harvest not only pumpkins, but carrots also, as shown in this simple stitchery and patchwork quilt! Have fun embroidering with the feather stitch and stem stitch. Combine with easy patchwork to make this sampler quilt.

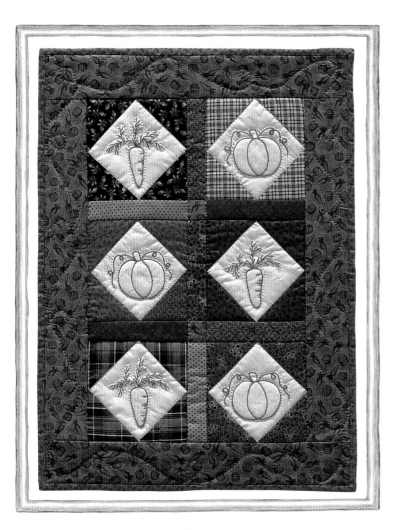

MATERIALS

- 14" x 18" piece of muslin

- ¼ yd. total assorted brown, orange, and blue prints and plaids for blocks and sashing

- ¼ yd. blue print for border

- ¾ yd. for backing

- ⅛ yd. orange print for binding

- 18" x 24" piece of thin batting

- Orange and green embroidery floss

- Embroidery needle

- Water-soluble marker

45

FINISHED QUILT SIZE
16" X 22"

DIRECTIONS

Measurements include ¹/₄"-wide seam allowances.

Step 1 – Using a water-soluble marker, draw 6 squares, each 4" x 4", on the muslin rectangle. Leave a 1" space between the squares to allow for cutting after the embroidery is complete.

Step 2 – Use a water-soluble marker to trace the pumpkins and carrots on the diagonal of the muslin squares. Place the muslin on top of the design over a light table or against a sunny window to trace the designs.

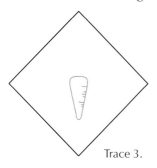

Trace 3.

Trace 3.

Step 3 – Embroider the carrots and pumpkins in a stem stitch, using 2 strands of orange embroidery floss.

Stem Stitch

Step 4 – Using 2 strands of green embroidery floss, embroider the carrot tops in a feather stitch, and the pumpkin vines in a stem stitch.

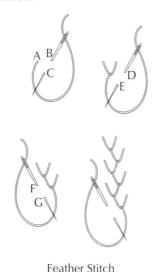

Feather Stitch

Step 5 – Cut the embroidered muslin squares on the drawn lines.

Step 6 – To frame the embroidery, cut 12 squares, each 3³/₈" x 3³/₈", from the assorted prints and plaids. Cut the squares once diagonally and sew matching triangles to the opposite sides of the muslin squares.

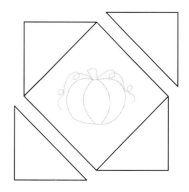

Step 7 – Cut 7 strips, each 1¹/₂" x 5¹/₂", from the assorted prints and plaids for sashing. Cut 2 squares, each 1¹/₂" x 1¹/₂", from the border fabric for the cornerstones.

Step 8 – Arrange the blocks, sashing strips, and cornerstones and sew them together.

Step 9 – Cut 2 border strips, each 2³/₄" x 17¹/₂", and sew to the sides. Cut 2 border strips, each 2³/₄" x 16", and sew to the top and bottom.

Step 10 – Layer the quilt top with batting and backing.

Step 11 – Baste and quilt as desired. We suggest quilting around the embroidered shapes and in-the-ditch around the blocks and sashing. Quilt a curved line to resemble a trailing pumpkin vine in the border.

Step 12 – Bind the quilt and add a label.

Embroidery Templates

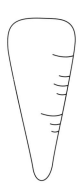

EMERSON'S DIVE TEAM

"It's a lot of work keeping all my ducks in a row," Emerson quacked.

"Okay, everybody—single file, wings back, bills down, flippers up, and no splashing!"

No one wants to get wet again after all the splashing those ducks did.
Come on, you yellow-bellied birds, start diving,
or someone's going to think you're chickens instead!

$\mathcal{E}$MERSON'S $\mathcal{D}$IVE $\mathcal{T}$EAM

his group was inspired by a single great find at a teddy bear show last summer—a 1940s child's bathing suit made in cream and butter yellow wool, with baby ducks appliquéd across the front.

Our first thought, of course, was: "This is perfect for Emerson, who else!" But the actual suit is being worn by our lifeguard, Sandy, whom it just fit. He's keeping a close eye on the baby ducks, along with trying to keep those nosy blue and yellow birds out of the way while the ducks dive.

CHICK

MATERIALS

- 1 craft-size square of yellow or blue wool felt

- Small scrap of orange wool felt

- Stuffing

- Orange floss

- 2 black round beads

- Hot glue

- 12" of 19-gauge wire

- Orange paint

52

This sweet blue bird is an easy first "stuffed animal" project.

DIRECTIONS

Step 1 – From the yellow or blue wool felt, cut:
- 2 chick bodies
- 1 chick gusset
- 4 chick wings
- 1 chick tail

From the orange wool felt, cut:
- 1 beak

Step 2 – With right sides together, sew the bodies from the small dot to the tail, using a $1/4$"-wide seam. Backstitch at each end.

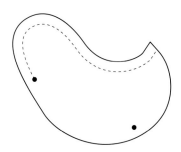

Step 3 – Fingerpress the seam open at the tail. Center the folded tail piece on the seam, with the shorter end of the tail facing the right side of the body, and the folded edge flush with the raw edge of the fabric. Tack in place.

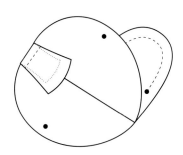

Step 4 – Sew the gusset to the body, matching the dots and stitching from dot to dot. Backstitch at each dot.

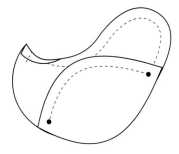

Step 5 – Sew from the tail to the large dot; backstitch.

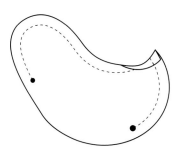

Step 6 – Sew from the large dot to the small dot, leaving 1¼" open for turning. Backstitch at each dot.

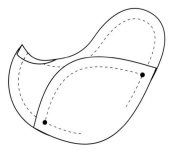

Step 7 – Turn right side out and stuff. Close the opening with a small overcast stitch.

Step 8 – Topstitch 2 wings together, ⅛" from the outside edge, then the other 2 wings.

53

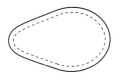

Step 9 – Sew the wings onto the body using the orange floss and a blanket stitch. Sew on the 2 black round beads for eyes.

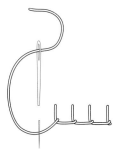

Step 10 – Attach the beak to the head using hot glue.

Step 11 – Cut 2 lengths of the 19-gauge wire, each 6" long. Using needle-nose pliers, make the first bend $1^3/4$" from one end of the wire at a 45° angle. From the point of the bend outward along the longer half, make 4 consecutive side-by-side 90° bends, $5/8$" apart. Paint orange; let dry. Attach to the chick by poking the legs upward into the body.

54

Templates

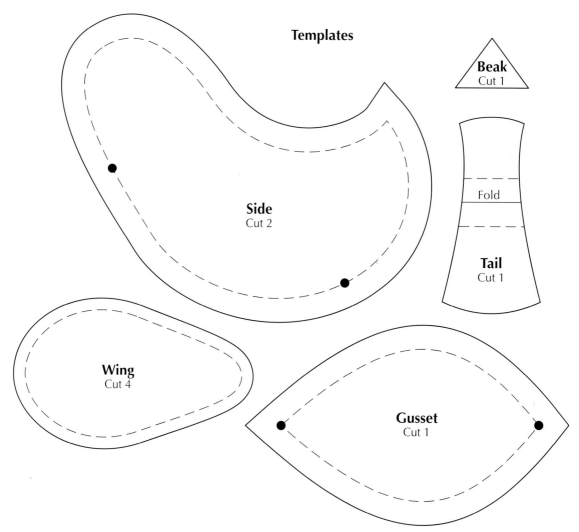

Beak
Cut 1

Side
Cut 2

Fold

Tail
Cut 1

Wing
Cut 4

Gusset
Cut 1

Sweet and simple nine patch Quilt

Fresh looking, easy to make, and fun to use describe this antique doll quilt.

Materials

- ³/₈ yd. total assorted solid and floral pastels for blocks

- ¹/₈ yd. yellow solid for border

- ⁵/₈ yd. for backing

- ¹/₈ yd. for binding

- 18" x 23" piece of thin batting

55

Directions

Measurements include ¹/₄"-wide seam allowances.

Step 1 – Cut 180 squares, each 1¹/₂" x 1¹/₂", from the assorted solid and floral pas-tels. (Or use the strip-piecing method shown on page 17, cutting strips 1¹/₂" wide.)

FINISHED QUILT SIZE
15" X 18"

Step 2 – Arrange the squares into Nine Patch blocks and sew them together. Make 20 blocks.

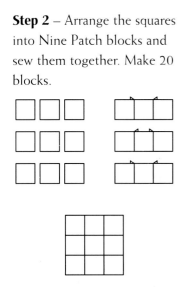

Step 3 – Sew the blocks together in 5 rows of 4, then join the rows to make the quilt top.

Step 4 – Cut 2 border strips, each $1^3/_4$" x $15^1/_2$", and sew to the sides. Cut 2 border strips, each $1^3/_4$" x 15", and sew to the top and bottom.

Step 5 – Layer the quilt top with batting and backing.

Step 6 – Baste and quilt as desired. We suggest cross-hatch lines through the blocks and into the border.

Step 7 – Bind the quilt and add a label.

57

CRICKET'S CLOSET

What are little girls made of?

Well, Cricket says it's what you wear, not what you're made of, that matters.

"Filling my shoes with lovely potpourri
will make my feet smell so sweet."

CRICKET'S CLOSET

**O**ur little bunny is as quick as a wink. In no time at all, she can be dressed all in pink. Her little-girl wardrobe was created with soft silks, sheer gauzes, flouncy chiffons, shiny satins, pastel organdies, and ruffled tulle.

Cricket's accessories, which, of course, just make the outfits, are darling wool-felt Mary Jane slippers in coordinating colors, flouncy floral bonnets, and European straw hats decorated with ribbons and bows that tie daintily under her furry chin.

61

PETITE SHOE SACHET

MATERIALS

- 5" x 6" piece of black felt

- 6" of ½"-wide green rayon ribbon

- Vintage pink carnation (or 1½"-diameter flower of your choice)

- 10" square of green tulle

- ½ cup lavender potpourri

- Pink and green embroidery floss

- Embroidery needle

- 1 button, ⁵⁄₁₆" diameter

62

Cricket's felt Mary Jane shoes make a perfect container for a fragrant lavender sachet.

DIRECTIONS

Step 1 – Cut 1 shoe sole and 1 shoe top from black felt. Cut 1 strip, ½" x 3¾", from black felt for the strap.

Step 2 – Sew one end of the strap to the inside of the shoe top at the placement mark.

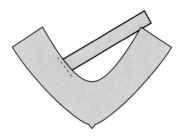

Step 3 – Sew the back of the shoe top together, using a ¼"-wide seam.

Step 4 – With right sides together, pin the sole and top together, matching the notches at the front and matching the notch at the back to the back seam. Sew, using a ¼"-wide seam. Turn right side out.

"Making your bed is so much more fun when you're wearing the right attire!"

Step 5 – Make a small bow, using the 6" of green ribbon. Glue the bow to the toe of the shoe, then glue the vintage flower on top of the bow.

Step 6 – Put potpourri in the center of the tulle. Draw up the edges of the tulle around the potpourri and tie with green embroidery floss, making a small bow.

Step 7 – Stuff the tulle bag inside the shoe.

Step 8 – Trim the end of the strap to a point. Sew a button to the end and through the side of the shoe with pink embroidery floss.

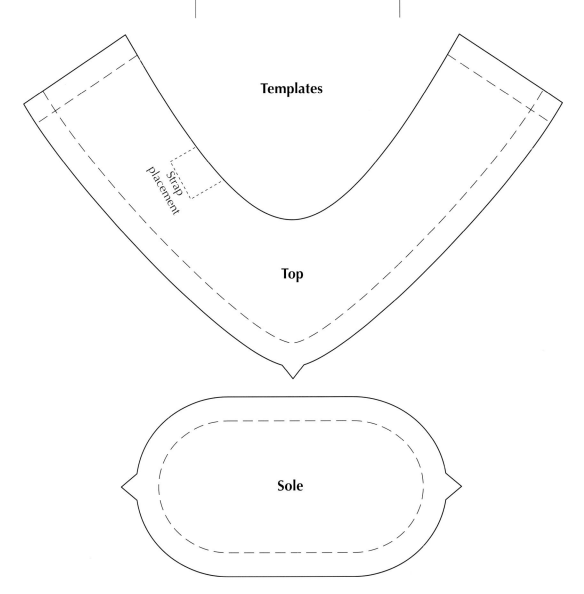

Templates

Strap placement

Top

Sole

Secret Garden Quilt

Soft pastel floral fabrics combine to make this dreamy quilt perfect for any setting. Tea-dyeing adds to its charm!

MATERIALS

- ³/₈ yd. total assorted pastel prints for Nine Patch blocks

- ¹/₂ yd. total assorted off-white floral prints for background, side and corner triangles, and binding

- ¹/₄ yd. pink print for border

- ³/₄ yd. for backing

- 22" x 26" piece of thin batting

65

DIRECTIONS

Measurements include ¹/₄"-wide seam allowances.

Step 1 – Cut 180 squares, each 1¹/₂" x 1¹/₂", from the assorted pastel prints. (Or use the strip-piecing method shown on page 17, cutting strips 1¹/₂" wide.)

FINISHED QUILT SIZE
20¹/₂" X 24³/₄"

Step 2 – Arrange the squares into Nine Patch blocks and sew them together. Make 20 blocks.

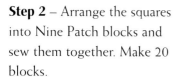

Step 3 – Cut 12 squares, each 3¹/₂" x 3¹/₂", from the assorted off-white prints.

Step 4 – Cut 4 squares, each 5¹/₂" x 5¹/₂", from the assorted off-white prints. Cut the squares twice diagonally for the side triangles.

Step 5 – Cut 2 squares, each 3" x 3", from an off-white print. Cut the squares once diagonally for the corner triangles.

Step 6 – Arrange the Nine Patch blocks, off-white print squares, and the side and corner triangles in diagonal rows and sew them together.

66

Step 7 – Cut 2 border strips, each 2" x 21³/₄", and sew to the sides. Cut 2 border strips, each 2" x 20¹/₂", and sew to the top and bottom.

Step 8 – Layer the quilt top with batting and backing.

Step 9 – Baste and quilt as desired. We suggest quilting a star in each of the off-white print squares, and a wavy line in the border.

Step 10 – Bind the quilt and add a label. If desired, tea-dye your quilt to soften its look.

Quilting Template

A
ꝼAMILY SUNDAY
ꝐICNIC

Why do they always have their picnic on a Sunday?

Because someone told them it wouldn't rain . . . that's why they call it a Sun-Day!

"No one has nibbled a bite today," Lolly said.
"Oh well, more for me then."

A Family Sunday Picnic

What better way to enjoy a delightful Sunday than at a family picnic, where you can share yummy food, play games, and wear your favorite weekend outfit. Everyone is dressed in fresh colors of watermelon pink and apple green.

71

The fabrics used for the group's outfits are new but have been made to look old-fashioned by dyeing them with tea and laundering them gently. A small rabbit print, solid cotton flannels, and crisp vintage linens make this charming group of picnickers a cheerful sight to behold.

Straw Hat

MATERIALS

- 7" straw hat

- 1 bias strip, 1" x 22$\frac{1}{4}$", for hat brim

- 2 bias strips, each 1" x 6$\frac{1}{2}$"

- 1" x 6$\frac{1}{2}$" piece of fabric

- 28" of mini-rickrack

- 6 buttons to cover, $\frac{3}{8}$" diameter

- Scraps of fabric for yo-yos, leaves, and buttons

- 50" of green cotton-covered craft wire (30 gauge)

- 2 yds. of $\frac{3}{8}$"-wide ribbon

- Craft glue

72

DIRECTIONS

For a vintage look, tea-dye or coffee-stain the fabric and bias strips. Soak fabric in water with tea or dissolved instant coffee until desired look is achieved. Do not rinse, and carefully wring out excess moisture. Let dry and press.

Step 1 – To attach the 22$\frac{1}{4}$" bias strip to the edge of the hat brim, stitch from the underside of the brim first,

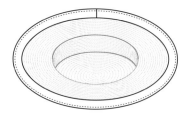

using a $1/4$"-wide seam. Turn the fabric over the brim, fold the raw edge of the bias strip under $1/4$", and sew in place.

Step 2 – Fold each of the $6 1/2$" bias strips in half lengthwise, wrong sides together; press. Open the pressed strip, fold each long edge toward the center fold, and press again. Sew a folded strip to each side of the $6 1/2$" fabric strip to make a hatband.

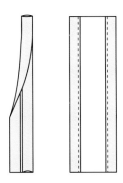

Step 3 – Pinch the ends of the hatband together and sew to the crown of the hat.

Step 4 – Cut the rickrack into 1 piece, 16" long, and 2 pieces, each 6" long. Make 2 bows from the 6" pieces of rickrack. Sew a bow at each end of the hatband.

Step 5 – Cover 2 buttons, following package directions. Sew a button on top of the knot of each rickrack bow.

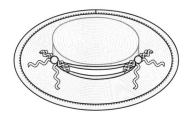

Step 6 – To make the yo-yos, cut 3 circles from fabric, using the circle template on page 74. Sew a running stitch $1/4$" from the edge of the circle. Pull the

thread to gather the circle into a yo-yo.

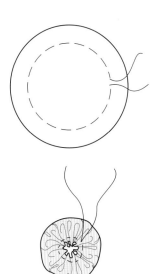

Step 7 – To make the leaves, cut 6 leaves from fabric, using the leaf template on page 74. Fold the leaves in half and stitch the rounded ends. Turn right side out. With the seam on the under-side, gather the raw edges of the leaf. Sew 2 leaves to the back of each yo-yo. Cover

3 buttons. Sew a button to the center of each yo-yo.

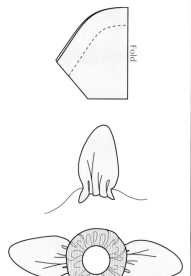

Step 8 – Cut a 16" piece of green wire, fold it in half, and stitch each end to the underside of a yo-yo flower. Cut an 18" piece of ribbon and set it aside. Wrap another piece of ribbon around the wire to cover it. Repeat the process with another 16"-long piece of wire, leaving one end without a yo-yo. Cover a 7" piece of wire with ribbon. Do not

add flowers; just stitch the ends of the ribbon to secure.

Step 9 – Make a double bow, using the 18" ribbon. Make a single bow, using the 16" of rickrack. Cover 1 more button.

Step 10 – Using a small piece of wire, wire together the double bow, rickrack bow, 9" of green wire, and the covered button.

Step 11 – Wire the center of the ribbon-covered wires to the back of the bows and button.

Step 12 – Glue the ribbons and bows to the hatband.

Step 13 – Twirl the ends of all the wires to make curlicues.

Templates

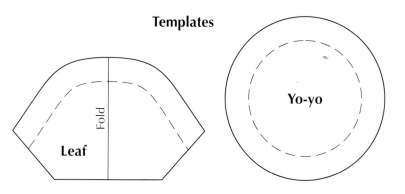

Leaf

Fold

Yo-yo

74

Garden Fence Quilt

This variation of the Rail Fence quilt block gives the illusion of the green grasses showing through the muslin "fence pickets."

Materials

- ½ yd. total assorted green prints, plaids, and checks for blocks

- 1½ yds. muslin for blocks, outer border, and backing

- ⅛ yd. pink solid for inner border

- ¼ yd. green print for bias binding

- Assorted pink scraps for yo-yo flowers

- ⅛ yd. green solid for leaves

- 24" x 32" piece of thin batting

- Ecru embroidery floss

- Embroidery needle

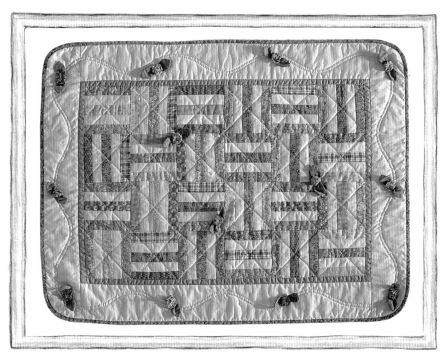

75

Directions

Measurements include ¼"-wide seam allowances.

Step 1 – Cut 24 strips, each 1¼" x 15", from the assorted green fabrics. Cut 16 strips, each 1¼" x 15", from the muslin.

Step 2 – Sew 5 strips together, beginning and ending with a green strip. Press the seams after sewing each strip. Make 8 strip

FINISHED QUILT SIZE
22½" X 30"

units. Cut the strip units into 24 blocks, each 4¼" x 4¼".

Make 8 strip units.

Step 3 – Arrange the blocks in 6 rows of 4 and sew them together. Join the rows to make the quilt top.

Step 4 – For the inner border, cut 2 pink strips, each 1" x 23", and sew to the sides; cut 2 pink strips, each 1" x 16½", and sew to the top and bottom.

Step 5 – For the outer border, cut 2 muslin strips, each 3½" x 24", and sew to the sides; cut 2 muslin strips, each 3½" x 22½", and sew to the top and bottom.

Step 6 – Use a small plate as a guide to mark the rounded corners on the quilt top. Cut along the marked line.

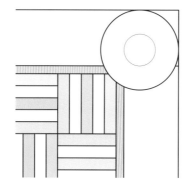

Step 7 – Layer the quilt top with batting and backing.

Step 8 – Baste and quilt as desired. We suggest quilting an "X" in each block, and a double wavy line in the border.

Step 9 – Cut bias strips from the green print fabric. Bind the quilt and add a label.

Step 10 – To make the yo-yo flowers, mark and cut 13 circles from the assorted pink scraps, using the circle template on page 77. Turn under the outside edge of the circle ¼". Sew ⅛" from the folded edge with a large running stitch. After stitching around the circle, pull the thread to gather the edges. Make a knot to secure the gathers. To hide the end of the thread, feed the needle through the fold and bring it out before cutting the thread.

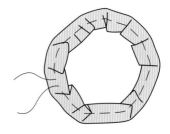

Step 11 – To make the leaves, mark the sewing line for 13 leaves on the wrong side of the green solid, using the leaf template below. Layer 2 pieces of green solid together and sew on the drawn line around each leaf. Trim ⅛" from the seam line. Cut a small slit in the center of the leaf and turn right side out. Press each leaf.

Step 12 – Gather each leaf at the center and attach a pink yo-yo flower. Sew the flower and leaf to the quilt with ecru embroidery floss.

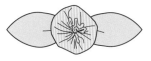

Templates

Leaf
Do not add seam allowance.

Yo-yo
Do not add seam allowance.

Little Quilt Primer

ROTARY CUTTING

You can use a rotary cutter, an acrylic ruler, and a mat to accurately cut several layers of fabric at one time. These tools, which can be purchased at quilt shops and fabric stores, are invaluable for making multi-fabric quilts.

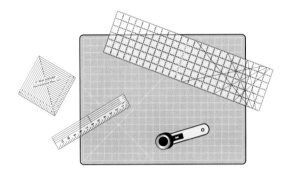

MACHINE PIECING

Use a $1/4$"-wide seam allowance. Often, what we think is a $1/4$"-wide seam allowance is too wide or too narrow. Use a ruler or graph paper to check. Set the stitch length at 10 to 12 stitches to the inch and use a neutral thread color. Since seams will cross each other, backstitching is unnecessary.

Pattern pieces are shown actual size and do not include any seam allowance. Add $1/4$" around each piece.

HAND PIECING

Step 1 – Make a template of each pattern piece. Transfer grain-line markings to your templates.

Step 2 – Place a template on the wrong side of the fabric, aligning the grain-line arrow with the grain of the fabric. Using a sharp pencil, trace around the template. The line you've drawn is the actual sewing line.

Step 3 – Add the seam allowance by cutting out the piece $1/4$" beyond the sewing line.

Step 4 – Pin the pieces together, matching the seam lines. Sew on the lines, using a small running stitch. Sew only from one seam intersection to another so that seam allowances remain free. Trim seams to $1/8$" after pieces are sewn together.

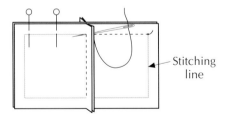

Stitching line

QUILTING

Step 1 – Mark quilting lines lightly with an ordinary pencil, washable fabric marker, or white pencil.

Step 2 – Cut the backing fabric and quilt batting a few inches larger than the quilt top all the way around.

Step 3 – Layer the backing, batting, and quilt top. Baste the layers together.

Step 4 – Quilt, using small, even stitches through all layers. Hide beginning and ending knots by pulling them gently through the quilt top into the batting.

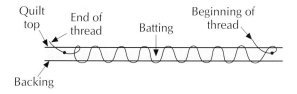

BINDING

Step 1 – Trim away excess batting and backing fabric from the quilt.

Step 2 – Cut strips of fabric for the binding 1¼" wide across the width of the fabric. Sew together enough strips to go around the quilt plus 4" to 5".

Step 3 – Place the binding on the quilt top with right sides together and raw edges even. Sew through all layers, using a ¼"-wide seam allowance.

Step 4 – Stop stitching ¼" from the corner, backstitch, clip the threads, and remove the quilt from the machine. Fold the binding up, then bring it down. Stitch from the edge as shown. Repeat at each corner.

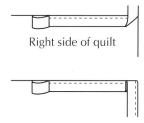

Right side of quilt

Step 5 – When you reach the starting point, sew the end across the beginning fold. Cut off excess binding. Bring the raw edge to the back of the quilt, fold under ¼", and blindstitch in place, covering the machine stitching.

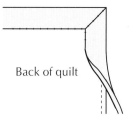

Back of quilt

Resources

Bunnies By The Bay
Office/Workshop:
3115 V Place
Anacortes, Washington 98221
Phone: (360) 293-8037
Fax: (360) 293-4729
E–mail:
bunny@bunniesbythebay.com
Internet:
www.bunniesbythebay.com

Retail stores:
2320 Commercial Avenue
Anacortes, WA 98221
(360) 299-9194
1-877-HOPS-2-IT
617 East Morris Street
La Conner, WA 98257
(360) 466–5040
1-888-BAYLEEE

The Little Quilt Magic Collection of fabric designed for Peter Pan Fabrics is available worldwide. The office and retail store are located at the address below. They invite you to visit and "step into our world." For catalog and mail-order information, send $2 to:

Little Quilts
1450-C Roswell Road
Marietta, GA 30062
Phone: (770) 578-6727
Fax: (770) 509-9748
Internet: www.littlequilts.com

The following books from Martingale & Company offer information on basic quiltmaking techniques and more:

Little Quilts All Through the House
Celebrate! with Little Quilts
Living with Little Quilts

The Authors

Bunnies By The Bay

Krystal Kirkpatrick and Suzanne Knutson have been sisters for over 40 years and business partners since 1986, when they first began their venture in the bunny world. They collectively create and bring to life over 60 new bunnies, bears, and a host of different friends twice a year. In 1996, they won their first national Teddy Bear Award with a sweet little bear named Alice, and a second one in 1998 with a little bear and her puppy named Olive and Wags. Exciting new ventures for Krys and Suzanne in the very near future include a wonderful fabric line, music boxes, figurines, snow globes, and, most important, a storybook line about the tales of Bunnies By The Bay and all their friends.

Little Quilts

Alice Berg, Mary Ellen Von Holt, and Sylvia Johnson have been designing and publishing booklets and patterns for Little Quilts since 1984. Each brings individual talents to the business, with sharing and compromise being their secret ingredients for success. They are the authors of three best-selling books from That Patchwork Place—*Little Quilts All Through The House*, *Celebrate! with Little Quilts*, and *Living with Little Quilts*.